How to Write a Children's Book in 30 Days or Less!

How to Write a Children's Book in 30 Days or Less!

▼

Stop Procrastinating and Start Writing Today

Caterina Christakos

Writers Club Press

New York Lincoln Shanghai

How to Write a Children's Book in 30 Days or Less!
Stop Procrastinating and Start Writing Today

Writers Club Press
an imprint of iUniverse, Inc.

For information address:
iUniverse
2021 Pine Lake Road, Suite 100
Lincoln, NE 68512
www.iuniverse.com

Illustrations (c)2002 Art Today

ISBN: 0-595-26260-0

Printed in the United States of America

CONTENTS

PREFACE

The first time I attempted to write a children's book, it took me three months (along with several years of promising myself that I would do it "one day"). In that time, I managed to wash the dog a million times, rearrange my closet, get my apartment so clean that they should have done a commercial about it, and procrastinate in ways that gave the word a new meaning.

When I actually sat down to write the book, it took me two days—and that was *with* editing. That is the longest it has ever taken me to actually write a children's book.

In reality, unless you are writing an epic, it will not take you longer than that period of time to write yours, either.

Why then the title, "How to Write a Children's Book in 30 Days or Less?"

So that you will have the time to wash the dog, clean the closets, and get Mr. Clean to personally come over and interview you.

Good luck, and enjoy your newfound career as a children's book writer!

Sincerely,

Caterina Christakos

P.S. If you ever have any questions, please feel free to email me at:

CChrist896@aol.com

I am always happy to help my fellow writers.

Back Up! Back Up! Back Up!

Normally, I would save this part for the end of the book, as most writers do, but I want to rescue you from making some of the same mistakes that I made.

My first book ever was half-written and about a hundred pages long. It wasn't a children's book, but a collection of memories from a particularly painful part of my life.

I had finally healed enough to begin writing and I was on a roll. But just as I was about to save a copy to my computer, disaster struck! One of our infamous Florida lightning storms hit and three hours of work, three pots of coffee, and my entire hard drive went right down the tubes.

My point? Save as often as possible and keep a backup copy handy. Back up what you are writing to your desktop and burn it onto a CD-ROM every five minutes! CD-ROMs are very inexpensive and they're worth their weight in gold. Most new computers have CD burners installed in them, and for those of you who have older computers, you can buy a fairly inexpensive external burner from Best Buy or Brandsmart. Don't let yourself fall into the habit of thinking that saving it to your hard drive alone is enough protection. Take it from my experience: you need this added pre-caution.

If your method of creative writing relies on pen and paper, photocopy your work twice a day. The dog could get to it or the kids may decide that it is their new coloring book.

Any way that you look at it, your work is too precious to lose due to laziness. Take the time to protect it, so that children everywhere can enjoy it for generations to come.

The Problem

The Problem That Most Writers Face

"Edison failed 10,000 times before perfecting the incandescent light bulb. Don't worry if you fail once!"
—Napolean Hill

The problem that most writers face is that they picture editors and publishers rejecting them before they have even written a single line of text. As Daniel Olson, an NLP specialist, once told me, "You are letting your critic come in way too early."

You are allowing the fear of a single possibility stop you from achieving your dreams. How will anyone have the opportunity to reject or accept your manuscript if you won't even write the first line?

You have done a great job of imagining the worst case scenario. Now let's use that incredible imagination of yours to imagine the best case scenario—your book being welcomed by at least one publisher or you taking the initiative to self-publish.

Many well-known, best-selling authors started with vanity or print on demand publishers and were later picked up by major publishing houses.

So let's look at your future as a children's book writer again. Has it gotten a bit rosier? Good. By the end of this book, you will be able to get your book written and published without any bothersome fears or insecurities getting in your way.

The second insecurity that I hear new writers express is that they don't know where to start. By the time you are finished reading the first chapter of this book, you will have more ideas than you know what to do with. So, if we are done with the concerns, excuses, and what ifs, let's get down to the business of writing!

Quotes from Famous Writers

And just in case you believe you are the only writer who has ever had doubts:

Our doubts are traitors, And make us lose the good that we oft may win, By fearing to attempt.
—William Shakespeare

When I face the desolate impossibility of writing 500 pages, a sick sense of failure falls on me, and I know I can never do it. Then gradually, I write one page and then another. One day's work is all I can permit myself to contemplate.
—John Steinbeck

My aim is to put down on paper what I see and what I feel in the best and simplest way.
—Ernest Hemingway

Omit needless words. Vigorous writing is concise. A sentence should contain no unnecessary words, a paragraph no unnecessary sentences, for the same reason that a drawing should have no unnecessary lines and a machine no unnecessary parts.
—William Strunk, Jr.

Most writers regard truth as their most valuable possession, and therefore are most economical in its use.
—Mark Twain

I read and walked for miles at night along the beach, writing bad blank verse and searching endlessly for someone wonderful who would step out of the darkness and change my life. It never crossed my mind that that person could be me.

—Anna Quindlen

For a creative writer possession of the truth is less important than emotional sincerity.

—George Orwell

Writing a book is an adventure; to begin with it is a toy and an amusement, then it becomes a master, and then it becomes a tyrant; and the last phase is just as you are about to be reconciled to your servitude—you kill the monster and fling it...to the public.

—Sir Winston Churchill

Keep away from men who try to belittle your ambitions. Small people always do that, but the really great make you feel that you too can become great.

—Mark Twain

Asking a writer what he thinks about criticism is like asking a lamp post what it feels about dogs.

—John Osborne

THE SOLUTION

The Solution—How to Jumpstart Your Writing Career

I know that it seems easier to make that extra pot of coffee, read that good book that you have had in storage for the last ten years, and suddenly decide to make the kids Halloween costumes by hand, than it does to make yourself sit down and write. Believe me, I have been there.

Here are some simple tips to get you started:

1. **Set the coffee pot, from the night before,** so that it automatically brews at the time you have planned to start writing.

2. **Set a time to write.** "At 4:00 p.m. today, I am writing my first children's book." Mark it on the calendar. Put little notes in every room to make your subconscious pick up the message and hold you to it.

3. **Gather all snacks** that you will just have to have two minutes after you sit down, and have a little lunch or dinner prepared from the night before.

4. **Sit for ten minutes and let your mind go.** Write down whatever pops into your mind. If the only thing coming to mind is, "I can't do this," then write that down. It could be the beginning of a story about a young boy who doesn't think he is smart enough to win the school's science fair, or a kid that everyone thinks is too wimpy to be the track star.

5. **Create a treasure map*** of what your life is going to be like after you are a published author, before you begin. This is a great exercise to get you going!

    * Treasure Maps will be explained in full on the next page. They are by far my favorite writing and life-enhancing technique.

Treasure Mapping—Step by Step

Begin by creating a picture of the life that you want to live. This will include the story you want to write and the life you will have once your book is published.

1. Get a poster board from your local drugstore or Kmart.

2. Draw pictures illustrating how you would like your story to proceed–or, if you are still searching for a story line, draw a picture of yourself at your computer.

3. Add the cover of a writing magazine to the board, along with a picture of the talk show host that will interview you after you are discovered. Put as much detail as possible into creating a picture of yourself as a successful writer. Why, you may ask? Because if you can't picture yourself as a successful writer, you won't be able to keep your motivation strong.

Treasure Mapping Your Way to Success

What is a treasure map? It is a piece of presentation board or cardboard that has pictures of you doing what you would like to do for a living. You could post, for example, a picture of you and Oprah together, as if you were conducting your first interview. Or how about a picture of a bookstore, like the ones that you will be doing book signings at? There are a million scenarios that you can come up with.

I do this for every book and project that I start–and it works!

When I wanted to book my first role in a movie, I put together a board showing my head shot surrounded by stars, money, and the talk show hosts I wanted interviews with. That year I landed my first starring role in a movie, on my very first audition.

I have done something similar for every book that I have written, whether I knew the subject matter ahead of time or not. It actually inspires me to be more creative and to get them done. I promise that it will do the same for you.

Practical Examples

Treasure maps can be applied to any situation.

Ex. 1 A friend of mine had always dreamed of having her book of poems published. However, she didn't think anyone would pay good money for her work. The poetry market is a difficult one to break into and, besides, she didn't have time to write while working and taking care of the kids. I told her about treasure mapping and, after staring at me as though I had two heads, she decided to try it. A week later, her boss called her in and told her that the company was going to have her work from home for a few months.

There went her excuse of not having enough time to write! Upon hearing the news, her children gave her a copy of the Writer's Market, pulled out her notebooks of poems, and lectured her about going after her dreams. Thirty days later, she had her book organized and edited and submitted to an online publisher. Her church heard about her endeavor and ordered thirty copies for their next festival. They all sold.

Ex. #2 Another friend that was in the position of owning a house that she wanted to sell, used a treasure map to get that house sold within a week. She had had it on the market for months, without so much as a nibble.

Finally, she created a treasure map with a picture of her house on it. She pasted a sold sign in the corner, and below the picture she wrote the exact amount that she wanted for the house. That day she received an offer, and by the end of the week she signed a contract for THE EXACT AMOUNT that was on her treasure map!

Ex #3 I told another friend of mine about this technique. At first she felt a little silly about it, but she was in some serious trouble at work. She was stuck in a job that she hated, was underpaid, and had a boss that kept hitting on her. I told her to make a board of herself doing a job that she loved. Within three weeks, she was laid off with a full benefits package and ended up receiving three job offers the very same day! Her phone has been ringing off the hook with calls from employers ever since!

Make your board and stick it by your bed or by your computer. It has to be somewhere where you see it often, so that you can ingrain your future success in your mind. Life wants to give you everything that you have always dreamed of; you just have to let life know what you want.

This method does work! Try it and see for yourself.

Practical Necessities:
The Basics of Targeted Writing

<u>Doing Your Research: Know Your Market</u>

Before you decide upon the type of book that you want to write, know your market. What do publishers in that area want? What are they looking for right now? Don't know? Don't worry. There are sources out there that will tell you exactly what publishers want.

If, on the other hand, you have no clue what you want to write, you can still use the same sources to gather ideas for books that publishers are actually clamoring for. You may have the greatest idea for a book about a family of beavers that shows children what life is like from their perspective. If there is not enough interest, though, or if the market is saturated with similar stories, your chances of getting published then diminish.

Here are some resources that will tell you exactly what publishers across the country are looking for:

1. **The Children's Writers and Illustrator's Market** is the Bible of Children's Book Resources. It lists all the editors that are looking for children's books and, more importantly, *exactly* what they are looking for. I have found several ideas for books simply by flipping through this wonderful resource.

2. **A second resource is your local library.** Go to your library and ask the librarian what types of books are

the most popular with children today. She will know what books are checked out the most and which children's book readings are the most popular.

She will also be a great contact for later, when you are looking to do your own readings in libraries. The library market is a large and lucrative one. Cultivate as many contacts within the library industry as possible.

3. **Go to the local bookstores and ask the people at the resource desk** which children's books are sought out the most and which have been their biggest sellers. Again, these people are wonderful contacts for later, when you are ready to do book signings. Fortunately, many bookstores are extremely receptive to helping out local talent.

4. **Read as many writing magazines as possible.** Many list monthly updates on what editors are looking for.

There are also paying contests you can enter to get your work noticed and critiqued at a very reasonable price. Winning some of these contests can build your name recognition and lead to contracts with some of the big publishing houses. Plus, you will get quotes from some top magazines to put on your book.

5. **Go Online.** There are tons of free resources online where you can get information. Go to writing chat rooms and message boards. There are also newsgroups on the net dedicated to writing and publishing. Go to writers forums and chat with others, all over the world,

who are either just starting out or who have already been published. Most people will be more than happy to answer your questions and offer support.

6. **Talk to your children, the neighbor's children, your nieces and nephews,** and anyone in the age range that you wish to write for. Ask them what their favorite books are. You can even make it a family project and have them help you come up with story ideas and characters. Kids are amazingly creative. They will come up with characters and story lines that you would never dream of. Plus, as an added bonus, they will be your best test market once your book is done.

   Here is a tip: If they say, "That's nice, mom," it isn't good enough. It is only when they can't put the book down that you know you have a winner.

How to Write for the Right Age Group

The number one question I get asked is, "How do you know which age group you are writing for?" You have to know this for submitting to editors and, more importantly, for developing your story line.

The answer lies in the stages of child development.

Children have different abilities depending on their age group. Picture books, for example, need to have simple concepts, because the children reading them take things very literally. Use very simple statements. A child between ages seven and nine can understand and process a lot more information and even handle some chapter books.

When you are writing, you must keep in mind which age group will be reading it.

Here is a breakdown of the types of books that are appropriate for children at different stages of their development:

Ages 6 months to 2 years: These kids are into texture. Give them cloth books or books with different items that can be touched. They are just discovering their world, with all its sights, sounds, and colors.

Ages 2–5 years: You can start giving them very simple picture books or books that have moveable parts. Children at this age like to take things apart and see how they work. They are able to follow simple, one-step instructions.

Ages 5–7 years: The picture books can be a bit more sophisticated at this age. You can use slightly bigger words and even write informational-type products. These kids are beginning to enjoy problem solving and are just getting into reading. A good theme for this age group might be magic tricks.

Ages 7–9 years: Chapter books surface at around this age. Children now have much longer attention spans and are able to connect events logically.

Ages 9–12 years: Simple novels and nonfiction. They are really getting into reading. Interest and hobby development now begins, and by age 12 they are delving into the world of fiction. According to the National Network for Childcare, this is the age when they start discussing their future careers.

Ages 12 years and up: Young adult novels

Stop Your Critic Before it Stops You

Most of us have a little voice inside our heads whispering endless reasons why we cannot succeed.

It says things like:
- What if I'm not good enough?
- What if no one buys it?
- What if my ex-husband is right and it *is* a stupid idea?
- Who am I to think that I could write anything that anyone would want to read, let alone buy?

I've got news for you. None of us was born with this voice. As newborns, we didn't think, "Man I don't think I can reach those bells hanging over my bed," or, "What if no one likes me?" These are things that we gradually learned through the fears of those around us.

Were you really scared to climb upon your first bike, or was it your parents' fears for your safety creeping in? Given the choice of any life or career in the world, would you choose the one that you are in, or is fear stopping you from living the life that you deserve? Were you brought up to believe that safety and earning a "comfortable living" were all that you deserve to expect from life? Realize this: your soul needs to be fed just as much as your body does.

For each of the questions above, you need to develop counter-questions to see you through to achieving your dreams.

Here are a few of my favorites:

1) What if I never try?
2) What if they are wrong?
3) What if I could have written a number-one bestseller?
4) What if that next query letter is the one that can get my foot in the door?
5) What if the author sitting at those book signings, with all of those children looking on in wonder, could have been me?
6) How will my life be different if I don't do this?
7) What kind of example will I be setting for my kids if I don't do this?

Realize this: you have nothing to lose and everything to gain.

Worst case scenario, you get to spend wonderful afternoons coming up with characters and brand new worlds that make you and your family laugh. You get some time to just dream again. You leave behind a legacy that your children and their children will treasure. Wow, wouldn't that be horrible?

Best Case Scenario, you are the next J.K. Rowling and your stories are adored worldwide. Either way, by writing your book, you are 90 percent ahead of most of the population in achieving your dreams.

Don't just dare to dream. Dare to do!

Getting over Your Fear of Rejection

Most people are afraid to go after their dreams because they fear looking foolish or being rejected by others. Let us put this in perspective:

Thomas Edison failed over 10,000 times before perfecting the first electric light bulb!

What are a few rejection letters from editors compared to that?

When they spoke of building a machine that would allow man to fly, The Wright Brothers were thought to be insane, and yet today people fly every day.

If mankind is capable of transporting himself through the air from one end of the world to another and sometimes to outer space, is it really so hard to imagine that you can sit in the comfort of your own home and write a book that others will want to read?

Let's look at the worst case scenario. You write your first book and it flops. Has the world come to an end? Have all of your neighbors come over to flog you or berate you publicly? Will your family disown you?

I could be wrong, but I'm betting the answer to these questions is NO!

You put the book that hasn't been appreciated yet aside, for now, and write another one (and another and another) and submit them until someone finally realizes that your writing is the best thing since sliced bread. Or you take it upon yourself to self-publish and prove to editors and publishers that there is a market for your book after all.

Later in this book, I will teach you how to self-publish, market yourself and your book, and get reporters and TV hosts to call you in for interviews.

Then, when the big publishing houses see how well it is selling, they will come to you and offer you oodles of money to buy the rights.

NOW ON TO THE BUSINESS OF WRITING!

Start Your Story with a Zing!

Books and movies have a lot in common. If your first scene doesn't grab the audience's attention, they won't hang around. Some of my favorite stories start directly in the midst of chaos. Start with a problem, if you can, or in the middle of an action scene. Begin with something unusual or intriguing. Get them curious!

Example #1:

Picture a kitten that is about to fall off of a bookshelf because she has climbed up to get her ball of pink string. The poor thing has gotten her paw caught and is about to fall, when she hears her owner's voice from down the hall. Will she be saved in time?

What does that do to your emotions? Do you feel anxious for the kitten? Do you want to find out what happens next? If your objective is to write a great story and sell a ton of books, then you have to reach your reader's emotions.

Example #2:

Pam raced up the stairs to hide Peter's gift. He was going to flip when he saw it. It was one of only three homegrown purple dinosaur eggs in the whole world! Professor Smitty had given it to her for saving his prized teletransporter from being hit by his clumsy nephew's glass of grape juice. How was she going to keep him from finding it before his birthday on Monday? He had managed to find every one of her presents for the last five years.

If you present your reader with a problem at the beginning of a book, he will immediately begin trying to solve it. In most cases, he will keep reading to see if he was right.

Example #3:

Xander couldn't believe it! His father was a wizard and so was he. Wait until the kids at school heard. Talk about a family secret. He bet that William Van Snobbin's eyes would pop out.

Give the reader something wonderful and unusual. Set their imaginations on fire and they will come back for more.

Example #4:

Mr. Frecklepuss and Mr. McQuee went out to sea to see, you see, the land of make believe. They set sail upon the Fairy Queen, manned by more pixies than you've ever seen. Some blond, some blue, but all part green, as decreed by manifest of the Fairy Queen.

For older children, you can use lyrical text, or if you are writing a story that you want parents to have fun reading to their children, make it almost like a song. Dr. Seuss' books have stuck in our minds for generations because of the unusual pictures and lyrical phrases.

Example #5:

Aunt Bess kept caterpillars in her bathtub and an owl by her bed. If you are writing a story for boys, the image of a bathtub full of caterpillars will definitely win their attention. Boys like to gross each other out and to be grossed out. Hence the popularity of fake vomit, and Harry Potter's "every flavor jelly beans." Note: if you have the chance to try the one that tastes like dirt–DON'T!

How to Come up with Incredible Characters

There are many books out there about character development. They run several hundreds of pages and cost an arm and a leg, but they are one way to go. My method of character development is simple:

Use Common Sense.

1) Use what is in front of you.

Look at your family and friends and see if they remind you of anything. Because of his husky whiskers, my first Shakespearean teacher reminded me of a caveman or a husky walrus. Does your Uncle Arthur have whiskers, wear glasses, and walk with a little bit of a waddle? Turn him into a know-it-all beaver or a store clerk, at a bookstore that sells books that you can actually climb into and live out an adventure. Does your sister have a talent for jumping rope and blowing bubbles, with purple bubble gum? Maybe the heroine in your next book could do the same.

Is their a kid in your neighborhood that is always getting into trouble? Hmm, do you think that the creator of "Dennis the Menace" might have known one?

You can use your family and friends' talents and physical characteristics to come up with tons of characters. One hint, though—if you choose to make Uncle Charlie a slug or Aunt Emma a rhinoceros, keep it to yourself. They may not be thrilled with their induction into literary history.

2) **Look around you.**

So, you say that you are an only child, with no family or friends and a strong case of agoraphobia? Not a problem. Flip on the television, have the newspaper delivered through the slit in your front door, or turn on your computer and surf the net. Start scanning news articles to see what is going on in the world. Find that one feel-good story about a boy who saved his dog from a burning building in Nebraska, and write about it. Or write about a surgeon that had dyslexia as a child and taught himself to work past his disability and fulfill his dreams. For every piece of horrible news out there, there are some amazing triumphs of humanity that need to be exposed.

3) **Look outside of your species.**

Stories don't have to include human beings at all. Write about a dog that saves a family of chimps or a grasshopper that teaches a school of tadpoles how to live on land. Write about an alien that lands on earth and what he learns from or teaches our planet. How would his view of the world be different if the only creatures he met here were alligators? The possibilities are endless.

The excuse that you can't think of anything to write about doesn't hold water. The same can be said for those that complain that "all the good stories are taken."

If you have sat around for two days with nothing on your piece of paper but your name, then take your first idea and run with it. It may not be your first award-winning book, but it will be the one you treasure the most later on. If you think of the first book that you write as just for you, you will take a ton of pressure off yourself. Later, you can even look back at your first attempt and laugh as you realize how far you have come.

Creating Believable Characters

The more that you know about your characters, the more believable they will be to your readers.

Write down each character's background, whether it will go in the book or not.

Example: Pig from Kansas City:

Bio: Lived on Mr. Arthur's farm until he got swept away in a bail of hay. Has pink skin with one brown spot on his ear.

His mother, Carol Piglet, always warned him of the dangers in the big city. His father, Joseph Piglet, recounted all the exciting things that could be seen in bigger towns.

Farm friends nicknamed him Spot, which was confusing because that was also the name of the farmer's dog. He dreams of seeing the big city and ends up appreciating his home.

Favorite treat: Chocolate ice cream that has fallen off the farmer's table.

Least Favorite Activity: Running through the mud.

His arch rival is Beatrice the cat, which has been the case ever since he accidentally sat on her favorite mouse toy and crushed it.

A bit more interesting than, "Spot was a pig," isn't it?

This pig now has character. If we gave him an earring, he might have a little more of an attitude. If we made his favorite flower pansies, he might appear to be a bit more sentimental.

If you flesh all of your characters out a bit, it will help them have more life and make your writing go a lot easier.

You need to know your characters before your audience can know them. So what makes this pig tick? Is he sentimental about the pansies because they are his mother's favorite? How does this effect his language?

Is he a very polite pig or is he a bit gruff and self-conscious about the fact that he's a pig? Explore this early on and you can almost eliminate writer's block. Just going back to your notes on each character can get you back in the flow of writing your story.

Creating Engaging Dialogue

I have said it before and I will say it again, when you sit down to write—write. Don't worry about the little details. After you have written your next best-selling children's book (which is the one you are writing now), go back and pay attention to the patterns in the dialogue. For now, if you worry about finding the perfect words for each and every sentence, you will drive yourself and those around you nuts.

Some things to look for after you have written your first draft:

Each character needs to have his or her own unique voice and it needs to be consistent. For example, if you are writing a book about an underprivileged child and an upperclass child, their inflections and patterns of speech should be different. Think of The Prince and the Pauper. A prince would have a different way of speaking and viewing the world than a pauper would.

If you have a character with a stutter in your book, you need to keep it up throughout the book—until the ending when he overcomes it.

Consistency is the key when writing any type of book.

If you want your character to have a Brooklyn accent, call up a friend from Brooklyn and pay attention to the way he or she speaks. Listen to kids that are from that area of New York, or flip on the television and listen to a show that is filmed there. Each region of the country has its own speech quirks. In some areas, a child asks his mom for a "coke," and in others it's a "pop." It's the little details that can make the difference.

My point is that once you have selected your characters and can picture and hear them clearly, you have to get them across accurately on paper. You won't want to be there with an editor or a child saying, "I know that it is completely out of character for Joe the Hippo to say he wants grits, when he is from New Jersey, but he was just in a grits mood."

Make sure the language patterns fit the character and also make sure that the entire length of a given character's dialogue is consistent.

Keep the Reader Reading!

Think about the last good book that you read. What kept you reading it? I'll give you a one-word answer: suspense. The author made you want to read more. You started caring about the characters and wanting to know what would happen to them next. It is the same with children's books. The kids need to care about the characters and have a burning desire to make sure that everything they're going through turns out all right.

How do we do that? Well, that is a two-part answer. The first is to create believable characters. The second is to create tension in the book.

Examples:

Dougie the duck scrambled down the hill to get away from that darn cat, but his webbed feet kept slipping. He could practically feel Stanley's hot tuna breath on his neck.

Roger just had to make the team. He had been practicing all summer.

Mandy bit off her last nail. If she didn't pass this English test, her mother would ground her for a month. Then she'd never get to go to Camp Glory, with the rest of her friends.

Talk to kids about things that they understand. Every child knows the fear of getting into trouble, and many know what it is like to have a bully after them. These are characters with problems that kids can relate to.

Give the children a problem that they can relate to and keep them on the edge of their seats, wondering if everything will turn out all right. Once you have outlined the hero and villain's characteristics and history, you can come up with a believable problem or situation to create suspense.

Think of the problems faced by children in the age group you are writing for, and give them to your characters. They will begin to relate to your characters and subtly learn a lesson in the bargain.

Stop Writer's Block Cold

Some writers say that they want to, "Write and let it flow." This does happen sometimes and it is a high greater than you can imagine.

What happens when it stops flowing, though? In most stories, you will reach a point where the story line flows and the characters take on lives of their own. Sometimes, though, they can be stubborn, or your brain will just say, "I need a break." For those moments, you need to have a plan.

1) Take a half-hour break and immerse yourself in something completely different. Forget about your story completely. It may be that both you and your characters are tired and need a break. Go soak in a tub, have a cup of tea, or take a nap. It may be all that you need to get going again. You may even find that your greatest inspirations occur while you're at rest. Your unconscious can handle any problem if you give it a chance. If you have developed your characters enough, you may even hear them urging you to get back to work and telling you exactly what happens next.

2) For those more severe occasions, it is good to come up with an outline. Between "Okay, what have I written so far?" and "Where do I want this story to go?" you can sometimes pick up your train of thought again. Or you can try picturing the ending first and work backwards to fill in the blanks. This may sound strange but it works.

A friend of mine who studies the human brain for a living taught me that technique. He said, "**Picture the book already done.** Picture the ending, then look back at your present self and tell me all the things you need to do to get there. What steps will your story need to take to get from where you are now to where you want to be? Start from the last chapter, then the one before it, and the one before that, until you get to the beginning. Fill in as many details as possible until you begin to see the whole picture step-by-step."

Example:

Fact #1: You know that you want your hero to win the football game at the end, with the use of his amazing scientific gadgets.

Fact #2: You know that in the beginning everyone thinks he is a graceless geek.

What needs to happen along the way to make him into a hero?

————>Well, you know that at some point in the story he will need to invent some of these gadgets and convince the coach to use them.

————>He will also need some close friends to help him out along the way, and an antagonist or two telling him that his ideas are nuts.

————> That would lead me to believe that his personal bully may need to come to respect him in the end, or get his comeuppance.

————> The scene before that may be the bully telling him, yet again, that he doesn't belong in the game.

————> Maybe our hero gets discouraged and is about to give up, when his best friend comes in screaming that he is a genius. She has just jumped over the fence using his incredible jump-o-matic machine!

Do you see how looking at it from a different angle can actually add substance to your writing? It is a great way to jump-start your imagination again. It can also help you to see if the story is actually going in the direction that you had intended, or if you are getting bogged down in details. Describing the exact color of each of the character's hair may seem important to you, but it doesn't keep the story flowing.

No flow means no reader. Using this method can actually turn your story into a better story than you would have originally come up with via the "Let's start with Chapter One" technique.

Write Better Now!

After you have finished writing your book, and I do mean *after*, go through your work and come up with more colorful ways to phrase your sentences.

Now before we go on, I want to explain why I insist that this must wait until after you are finished with your first draft. If you spend your time nitpicking at your work while you are writing it, you will never get anything done. I have known writers who've gone into a full state of writer's block while trying to find that one perfect word. If that happens to you, put a blank line where the word needs to go and come back to it later. One word is not worth throwing off your whole writing flow. After your work is done, go back and spice it up.

Realize, though, that you are writing for kids, not for Shakespeare fans. Long words might impress your friends and a few literary critics, but they may turn off your true audience. On the next page you will find examples of simple ways to spice up your sentences. Many times it boils down to enhancing the readers' experience. You can give them a three-word sentence with "just the facts," or you can make it creamier, glowing, scrumptious, exhilarating, and a million other things that give your words and your story life. Draw your audience into the story by making it real for them. Help them to taste, smell, and feel what your characters are experiencing!

Here are some examples of simple ways to spice your sentences up:

1) The fox jumped over the fence.
   Better version:
   The fox leaped over the fence, avoiding the hound's snarling jaws by mere inches.

2) Nora was a pretty blond-haired girl.
   Better Versions:
   Nora's golden curls sparkled in the sun.
   The boys were mesmerized by her glistening blond hair.

3) Brownies are Nick's favorite dessert.
   Better Version:
   Nick loved the way the rich chocolate brownies melted on his tongue. He could eat them all day long.

Do you see how adding a verb or adding a more descriptive adjective can make all the difference in the world? You want that brownie to be so real that readers can practically taste it.

My advice—get a thesaurus and keep it by your computer at all times. Get a second one to put by your bed at night, along with a notebook for recording those breakthroughs that you will start to get at three in the morning.

Also, when you are eating your own brownies, take a second to truly experience them. When you lay out in the sun, feel the rays soak into your skin. And when you drive to work, really pick up on all the colors and scents you experience on the way. By being aware of your environment, you will be able to add depth and sensation to your writing.

Do you remember the story "Charlie and the Chocolate Factory"? The first time I read it, I could almost feel myself floating in a river of chocolate. I could practically taste the gum creating the taste of fresh pies melting on my tongue. If you haven't read that book, go out and buy it today. It is an excellent example of creating a visceral reality for readers.

Better Words

Here are some better word alternatives to get your imagination flowing:

Ran——————————> tore through, raced, bolted, leaped, sped, flew after his sister

Ate——————————> devoured, gulped, slobbered, tore into, consumed, wolfed, slurped

Danced——————————> swayed, bopped, twirled, waltzed, floated, pranced

Jumped——————————> leaped, catapulted, bounced, bolted over the fence

Bumped——————————> jarred, careened, knocked, slammed, bounced

Laughed——————————> giggled, chuckled, guffawed, snorted, belly laughed, wailed with laughter

Played——————————> messed around, frolicked, tousled, romped, amused themselves

The Real Test

Most people think that the real test of whether their writing is good or not is whether or not some editor in New York loves it. Before it even reaches that point of evaluation, there is an even better way to test your book. Read it out loud. How does it sound? Does it flow? A story can look great on paper, but if it does not read well, it could have some serious problems.

Imagine a mother or father reading it to their kids at night. Most children's books are bonding experiences between parents and children. If bonding moments are ruined because you haven't taken the time to read your book out loud, you can bet that they will never pick up that book again or recommend it to their friends.

If you don't have children of your own, you can always volunteer your time and read to underprivileged children in your community. It makes a world of difference to them and can be an extremely rewarding experience for everyone involved. Children are also pretty honest about what they like or don't like. If something needs to be changed, they will tell you more often than not. You may even see your story take off in a new and better direction because of it. Some other places that you can look into are your local library, schools, and hospitals. Children in hospital wings are stuck in one place all day long. Some children with more serious illnesses are there for months at a time, and it can be extremely boring. Trust me, I spent most of my childhood in hospitals, and the time that volunteers spent with us made all the difference in the world. There is nothing like hearing a great story to take your mind off your troubles and your pain.

List of Writers Magazines

The Writer
The Writer was founded in Boston in 1887 and has since been an invaluable resource for professional writers. For everything from learning how to use the Internet to get writing jobs to learning better writing techniques, it is a wonderful resource.

Book Magazine
Book Magazine is a newer magazine that focuses on what is being published right now. It gives updates on authors and the newest, hottest books on the market.

Writer's Digest Magazine
Writer's Digest Magazine is known as one of the leading publications for aspiring writers. It offers news on what editors are looking for right now, contests that you can enter, and tips on how to make your writing better and easier to publish.

Mosaic Magazine
Mosaic Magazine is devoted to all types of Hispanic and African-American literature. It focuses on the authors that are hot right now and the subjects that editors are looking for.

Children's Digest Magazine
Children's Digest Magazine is a wonderful source for children's book writers. It stays up-to-date with current industry trends, lists contests for children's writers, and tells what editors are looking for right now.

Children's Playmate Magazine
Children's Playmate Magazine has stories, articles, and poems for beginning readers ages 6 to 8.

Publisher's Weekly
Publisher's Weekly helps you stay in touch with what is happening in the publishing industry internationally. Early reviews of children's and adult literature are usually found here.

Publishing Your Manuscript Ironclad Rules

1) **Double space your manuscript.** Editors need to be able to make notes in the margins and between the lines. Plus, it helps them avoid eye strain while reading manuscript after manuscript.

2) **Write on one side of the page only.**

3) **Use white 8 ½ x 11 inch typing or computer paper.** No cutesy designs or recycled paper. This is their first impression of you, and you want to be perceived as a professional.

4) **Edit your work or have a professional editor edit it.** No typos or spelling errors allowed. They will not read your work if they see that you did not care enough to do so.

5) **Use a standard font, like Times New Roman.** Other fonts can be difficult to read. You want to make this process as painless for them as possible.

6) **Type it on a computer.** No handwritten manuscripts. If you must use a typewriter, make sure that it has a fresh ribbon.

7) **Always include a self-addressed stamped envelope (SASE),** so that they can return it to you. Many publishers will toss out your manuscript if you don't follow this industry standard.

How to Self-Publish Your Stories

Here are the pros and cons of self-publishing:

Pros:

1) Self-publishing can bring you anywhere between 30 and 70 percent of the profits. Most publishing houses pay less than 10 percent of the profits to the writer.

2) You maintain complete creative control. When you sign with a traditional publisher, you give away a lot of creative control.

3) You decide when your book starts to sell. Publishers have the right to buy your book and keep it in-house for a certain period of time. In other words, you may sign a contract and your book could sit in storage for a year. During that time you receive nothing, because you only get paid for copies sold.

Cons:

1) It will cost you more to produce a full color children's book. Publishers take care of that cost so you don't have to invest your own money.

2) If you can't draw, you will have to hire an illustrator. Publishers have their own illustrators. Again, they foot the bill.

3) You may have to work twice as hard to get your book noticed. Although you are still responsible for marketing your book, a traditional publisher may be able to put you in contact with the right people.

If you like to market and network and you enjoy working on your own, the self-publishing path is a wonderful choice. However, for those of you just starting out and in need of added guidance, submitting to publishing houses might be a better way to begin.

There have been times when I would have appreciated having a publisher to take care of all the details while I worked on my next book. On the other hand, I enjoy receiving bigger commission checks.

Everything in life is a tradeoff. Look at both options and see which one is right for you.

Types of Self-Publishing

Vanity Press: This is a publishing house that will publish your book for a fee, then either give you the profits or split the profits with you. In many cases, editing costs extra and you have to find your own distribution channels.

Print on Demand: You pay a setup fee and they print your book as soon as an order is placed. This means that you don't have to worry about storing them. Many of these companies have distribution channels set up. Many have connections with several online bookstores, like Amazon.com and Barnes and Noble. They will edit your book for you for a bit of extra money, and get you registered with Bowker. Bowker is the company that assigns your book an ISBN number so that stores can buy it.

This is how I published my last book, "How to Completely Blow Your Competition Away at Any Audition," and the publisher did a wonderful job. The editor that they assigned to me e-mailed me weekly to keep me up-to-date on its progress. They also designed the cover for me.

Creating Your Marketing Plan

—Here are just a few ideas. There are thousands of things you can do.

1. Put together a list of all the local, privately owned bookstores in your area.

2. Put together a list of the national chains in your area.

3. Get the names of the managers at each location.

4. Call each store ahead of time and let them know that you are coming in.

5. Arrange good times with the local stores (about 3 weeks in advance), to do book signings.

6. Call the local papers and let them know when you will be holding your book signings.

7. Talk to the national stores and see who you need to speak to about doing signings.

8. Find local writing groups in your community and offer to give lectures on how to write children's books. Bring copies along to sell. Again, promote this in your local paper.

9. Talk to your local librarian and offer to do a book reading at their library. Also, find out the procedure for having your book reviewed for purchase by the

library system. Again, bring extra books. If the kids like your story, the parents will buy it.

10. If your story has an educational theme, approach the public school system about either giving a talk or reading the book to the students.

11. Buy a mailing list of families in your area with kids of the ages that your book is geared to. Send them little postcards with pictures of your book, your photo, and an announcement of your next book signing on them.

How to Have Reporters Clamoring to Interview You

The Press Release and Press Kit

Basic Principle: You can't get interviewed if they don't know who you are.

Your Press Kit: Your Press Kit will contain several versions of your press release, your bio, your Q & A, any prior press clippings that you have, and a professional black and white photo of yourself.

The Press Release: Most people write the usual boring: Ms. So and So has just come out with her newest book. The question to ask, as publicity guru Paul Hartunian has said, is "Who cares?"

This may sound harsh, but unless you stimulate a reporter's curiosity, he or she won't be motivated to promote your book. Interviews are an exchange of services. You give them something interesting to write about, and they will be more than happy to plug your book.

Don't make the press release seem like an advertisement for your book or they will chuck it.

Ex. Jane Wood writes "Jane Goes To Mars."—BORING

Do people care about a new book by someone they haven't heard of? Probably not.

Ex. of better release: **10 Ways to Get Your Child to Read**

Do people care about getting their kids to read? Yes. So you give them ten ways to make reading fun for kids.

Within the press release, you must give them your credentials, which will include being the published author of "Jane Goes to Mars."

Congratulations! You have just become an expert on getting kids to read and you now have a reputation as a published author!

When you make the release and the story about them, they will want to know more about you. On the next page, I have included a sample press release. **Make sure that your release is on one side of one paper only. Double space it. And use only high quality paper and ink.**

FOR IMMEDIATE   FOR FURTHER
RELEASE   INFORMATION CONTACT
                  CATERINA CHRISTAKOS (407) xxx-xxxx

The Seven Survival Skills Every Actor Must Know
Truly talented actors and entertainers are passed over every day, while
actors without any formal training are granted incredible parts. Why,
you may ask? One reason stands above the rest. They know how to
audition.

"You can be the best actor in the world but if you don't know how to
audition your career is dead in the water," says Caterina Christakos,
actress, writer, and founder of the Audition Network.

Caterina is a powerful and entertaining interview subject. She'll tell
your audience:

a)   Seven secrets for blowing your competition away
b)   The biggest mistake most actors make at auditions
c)   Three Rules for Picking an Acting Coach
d)   Three follow-up Secrets that You Must Know

Caterina is an accomplished actress and model, as well as a published
author. She is currently starring in the feature film "Alone and
Restless," to be released in the Summer of 2003. She has learned from
her mistakes and can give your audience practical advice to make their
transition into the acting world a lot easier.

To schedule an interview, call Caterina at (407)970-2778

# # #

Little Things to Know

1) In the left-hand corner, put "For Immediate Release," if it doesn't really matter when they send it out. If, on the other hand, your book is related to Thanksgiving, you should put: For Release before Thanksgiving 2002.

2) In the paragraph at the bottom, include only those credentials of yours that apply to this book. If the book is about kids in a ghost town, don't mention your stint in the local theater. Your Ph.D. in geology probably wouldn't apply, either.

3) If you have someone other than yourself acting as your contact person, you may get more calls. As silly as it may seem, they will think that you are more of a professional if you have someone else taking your calls.

   Just make sure to train that person on what to say!

4) The symbol ### must be placed at the bottom of your release. It lets the reporter know that the press release is over.

Your Bio Sheet

Your bio sheet will, again, include only those accomplishments that pertain to your being an authority on getting kids to write. Mention your BA in English, if you have one. If you are the parent of two five-year-olds, then that is relevant. That, my friends, is hands-on experience. Obviously, if you have written anything else, include it. Naturally, include the name of your latest book, with a tiny blurb regarding what it is about.

Your bio sheet should be one page in length and to the point.

Your Q & A

Your Q & A is your question and answer sheet. This is another jewel that I picked up from Mr. Hartunian's PR course. When a reporter asks if you have anything else for them, you can say, "Yes I have a bio sheet and a Q&A."

The Q & A is a sheet with ten questions THAT YOU COME UP WITH, for the reporter to ask you. This eliminates the need to be nervous before interviews, because you have told them exactly what to ask you. You can therefore have the answers prepared way ahead of time!

Most people have no clue what these things are, so you are already way ahead of the game. For more help, I recommend that you get Paul Hartunian's course. Its information is invaluable for anyone interested in self-promotion.

* I don't receive any commission for mentioning his course. I just know that his information is *that* good!

Getting on Talk Shows

Once you start doing newspaper interviews, in many cases, local radio stations will begin to call. If you do well there, television stations will start coming around. Once you have done television, if you gave a good interview and your topic is interesting enough, the talk show hosts will find you.

There are ways to get on talk shows without going through this process. I donot recommend them, though, because you will need the experience of interviewing for these smaller shows first. If you screw up on a tiny show in the middle of nowhere, no one will care. If you screw up on "Oprah," you can kiss self-promotion goodbye for awhile.

Have several people that you know read your questions to you, and practice your answers. Have them throw in a few questions that are not on your Q & A, just in case. Polish your image so you will be ready when Oprah's staff calls.

Bonus Section

Quick Reminder of Writing Tips

Practice Writing Exercises

Creative Meditation Exercises

**30 Day Step-By-Step Guide to Writing—
Tells you exactly what to do every day**

Final Reminder—Quick Writing Tips

1. **Keep a pad and pen with you at all times.** You never know when inspiration may strike. I have nearly kicked myself several times because I had a great idea and no way to write it down. You almost always forget the important details if they are not written down immediately.

2. **Write down the positive and negative things that come to mind.** Your characters and story lines can be based on both. Help a character solve a problem you may be going through.

3. **Network.** Get to know as many librarians and bookstore managers as you can. Go to writers conventions. Form a writing group. These connections can prove to be invaluable later on.

4. **Talk to kids.** Children are your greatest resource, bar none. Ask them what they are interested in. What do they want to read about? If they were your characters, what would they do in different situations?

5. **Back up everything.** Accidents happen. It would be a shame to see all of your hard work go to waste.

6. **Read writers magazines constantly.** Stay on top of what is happening in your industry. Find out what editors are looking for right now.

7.   **Enter writing contests.** They are a great way to hone your writing skills, get advice from top professionals, and be seen by editors and publishers nationwide.

8.   **Keep a recorder with you in the car.** If you can spare the cash, get a voice-activated recorder for your car. You never know when inspiration will occur, and you don't want to lose it because you can't find a place to pull over and jot something down.

Writing Exercises

Here are some great exercises to warm up your writing muscles. Try them out whenever you feel the need to hone your writing skills or come up with new story lines.

1. **I will give you the beginning of a scene and you finish it.**

    - Jenny looked down at her dress. It was ruined! Looking up, she saw John laughing and she…
    - Tom couldn't believe his eyes. Right there in front of him was…
    - It had three heads and a long tail and it was coming right at them…
    - Grasshoppers in bed? How was she ever going to get any sleep?
    - Uh oh, Tim's dad looked mad!
    - Wow, what a mess. There was chocolate chip cookie dough everywhere…
    - As Marley waved his wand…

2. **I will give you several themes to write about.**

    - The best vacation I ever went on was…
    - My favorite class in school was _____ because…
    - The funniest thing I ever saw was…
    - The thing I love the most about my pet is…
    - The best book that I ever read was _____ because it made me feel _____…

3. **Pick one subject and brainstorm. Write down every single thing that comes into your head when you look at a given word.**

   Ex. **Popcorn**—movies, dating, popcorn fights, love, laughter, comedy, drama, actors, actresses, Catherine Hepburn, Tarzan, Carey Grant, Rocky, juju bees, projectors, digital, sadness, crying, happy, laughing, holding hands, kissing, concession stands, matinees, Star Wars, The Empire Strikes Back, aisles, cushy seats, gummy seats, soda, hotdogs, teenagers making out, horror movies, closing my eyes, snuggling, sneaking in, ticket stubs

   Now take any 5 of the words that you came up with and create a story from them.

4. **Flip through National Geographic and pick three animals.** Create a story around them. Ex. A lion, a snake, and a giraffe all want to be King of the Jungle. The lion because of ancestry, the snake because its bite is fatal, and the giraffe because it stands head and shoulders above the rest.

5. **Pick a part of the world that you have never been to.** Read as much as you can about it. Write a story about an exchange student from that country coming to America.

6. **Pick up a newspaper and write a story about the first good news story that you read.**

7. Read a comic strip and write your own version of it, using their characters.

8. Watch half of a child's video that you haven't seen before, then turn off the tape. Now create an ending for it.

9. Write a story in which a problem that your child is having is solved.

Creative Meditation or Cooperation

Here are some exercises to tap into your creative unconscious and your creative spirit. We all have the capacity for
genius. Scientists claim that we use barely 10 percent of
our brains' potential. We tend to get so involved with our
lives that we forget to just be. Inspiration comes when we
are silent or when we actively request it.

1. Physical exercise—Thomas Edison claimed that he
    did different exercises to help spark his creativity. He
    had a specific exercise for each type of project that he
    was working on. I like walking or driving my car. I
    have had amazing inspirations while doing both of
    these activities. I just let my mind go and suddenly,
    like a bolt of lighting, a fantastic idea hits me and I
    have to pull over and write it down.

    Have you ever been on the treadmill and had to jump
    off because you either remembered something or
    thought of some new way to solve a problem? Or have
    you ever been on a long trip and found that your mind
    had wandered so much that you couldn't remember
    driving so far?

    These are the times when your subconscious takes over
    and your best ideas can manifest themselves. Try walk-
    ing, or simply turn off the radio the next time that you
    drive. Any type of movement can get that creative
    energy flowing.

2. I have heard of creative geniuses who simply sit in rooms and let ideas come to them. They close all the lights, tell their loved ones to stay on the other end of the house, and just sit in the silence. Eventually, their minds settle down and inspiration drifts to them. We seem to be besieged with sights and sounds at all times. Giving yourself a break from the outside world gives your mind a chance to be still and listen up for those sparks of inspiration.

    When asked about it, Mozart claimed not to know where his music came from. He took no credit for it because he said it just came to him. Perhaps if we are open to it, our own creative genius will emerge.

3. Ask your unconscious a question about your story before you go to sleep. Instruct it to have an answer waiting for you when you wake up.

    Practice this every night for a week. By the end of that week, you may be surprised at what comes to you.

4. Form a mastermind group.

    What is a mastermind group? Loosely put, a mastermind group is a group of like-minded people who get together to brainstorm for a common purpose. Get a group of writers together and work on a single story, or spend time brainstorming about each author's next story. You can also form a group that helps to market all of your stories together as a package to publishers and the press.

5. **Go to a museum.** Go to an art museum, a science museum, or a history museum. Pick one exhibit and study it. Come up with a story about it.

6. **Sit at the beach.** Sit at the beach or in any type of natural setting. Let your mind wander as you relax. Write whatever pops into your head.

30 Day Step By Step Writing Guide

—How to Write and Still have a Life

DAY 1

Brainstorming day.

Write down a list of topics that you would like to write about. If possible, talk to children who are of the age that you would like to write for. Ask them what their favorite books are. Talk to them about the subject you are interested in and see if it is actually something that keeps their attention. If they act polite and tell you that that seems like a nice story, eliminate it from your list. The response that you are looking for is when they keep asking you questions about what is going to happen next. If they get excited and ask you dozens of questions, you are on the right track. Put a copy of your brainstorming list next to your computer.

Day 2

Get a blank video. (I'll explain on Day 7.)

Go to your local library or bookstore with a pen and paper. Find a copy of this year's "Children's Writers and Illustrators Market." Make sure that it is this year's edition. Editors change frequently.

Pick the topic that you would like to write about and the best age group your topic is for, as outlined in this book.

Scan the "Children's Writers and Illustrators Market" for any publishers and editors who publish work on that topic. Is there a great interest in it? If not, pick another topic. Put any notes that you take on your final subject by your computer.

Day 3

If you are still stuck on what to write about, go back to the bookstore and scan the writing magazines. There are always contests and publisher updates. Through these magazines, publishers and editors will announce what they are currently looking for.

Once you have chosen your subject, go to your local drugstore or Kmart and get a poster board. Also make sure that you have glue, scissors, and magazine pictures of the people and things that will be in your new life as a writer.

Day 4

Wash the dog.

Get your poster board, glue, scissors, and pictures out, and place them on your board in whatever way is visually appealing to you. Write key words around the picture, like writer, talk show, money, kids, book signings, and whatever else is meaningful to you. When you are done, place the finished product next to your bed. From now on, this will be the first thing you see in the morning and the last thing you see at night.

Day 5

Vacuum your entire house.

Call all your frequent phone buddies and relatives and tell them that you will be shutting the phone off at a certain time from now on. You are working on your writing and you know that they will respect that.

If any of them see you wandering around the market or mall at that designated time, they are required to guide you back home, straightaway!

Sit your family down and ask them to respect that time, as well. Any disputes will be settled after your writing is over.

Sandwiches will be available in the fridge, along with other necessities, so there will be no need to disturb you.

Day 6

Do the laundry.

Write down the exact time that you will be writing tomorrow. Post this info in every room of the house, and by your computer.

Make tomorrow's lunch and dinner ahead of time. See to it that the family has theirs as well.

Set the coffee maker to go off at exactly the time that you will start writing. Get to sleep early. You have a wonderful day ahead of you.

Day 7

Begin the day by staring at your board.

Take a deep breath.

Visualize yourself as a successful writer.

Take your blank tape from Day 2 and use it to program your VCR.

Your talk show, soap, afternoon news, or whatever else that you may watch will be recorded. No worries or distractions. You can watch your shows later.

Go to your desk and have a sip of your coffee. Review the notes and brainstorming that you did on Days 1-4.

Close your eyes.

What type of characters would live in the type of story that you are creating?
Is it an animal story?
Is it a kid story?
Is it a magic story?
Come up with an outline of your characters.

Write for 30 minutes only.
Set your coffee machine for tomorrow. You are done for today

Day 9

Grab your daily snacks and coffee.

Pull out your character list.

Come up with histories and characteristics for each character. Your concepts do not need to be written in complete sentences.

Ex.
Jeremy the Hedgehog—son of Alberta and Joseph Hedgehog
- furry with droopy brown ear
- bright but the class clown
- picked on by his brother Bill
- wants to be on the Hedgehog soccer team more than anything but he has a bad knee

Do this for each character, then stop.

Is there anything missing?

Analyze, add, and modify as needed for half an hour.

Day 10

Grab your cup of coffee and snacks.

Write a brief paragraph stating what you want this story to be about.

Look over your character descriptions. Do they fit in with your story line? If not, modify either the characters or the story.

Create an outline of what events need to occur to get from the beginning to the end.

What problem needs to be solved?

Day 11

Go to a park. Sit outside and let your mind go. Write down anything that occurs to you about your story.

Now go home and write.

Don't worry about spelling, grammar, or anything else.

Just write what comes to you.

One hour of writing tops for today.

Day 12

Review what you have written without criticism.

Is it going in the direction of your outline?

Adjust it accordingly.

Review the age group that you are writing for again.

Does your work fit in with that age group?

Again, adjust it accordingly.

Days 13-15

Continue with your routine until your story is done. If you run into a glitch, return to the section on getting past writer's block.

DO NOT THROW ANY OF YOUR WORK AWAY IN A FIT OF FRUSTRATION.

NO CRITICISM.

THINGS THAT MAY NOT WORK FOR THIS STORY MAY BE GREAT FOR ANOTHER STORY YOU MAY WRITE DOWN THE ROAD.

Day 16

Go back to the beginning of your story.

Look at the first sentence and the first paragraph.

Does it grab the attention? If not, adjust it.

Add some action.

Put the reader in the midst of suspense and stimulate a strong curiosity.

Review the page in this book called START YOUR STORY WITH A ZING.

If this is a chapter book, do this for the first sentence of the book and the first sentence of each chapter's first paragraph.

Day 17

Review your characters' dialogue.

Is it consistent?

Do they maintain their accents and mannerisms?

If not, go through each character's dialogue and adjust it.

Day 18

Read your story aloud to yourself. Does it flow?

This is the best way to find the rough spots.

Work on those rough spots today.

Have someone that is supportive and honest read your work.

Listen to their suggestions with an open mind. Their words are not gold but they may be a good lead for further improvement.

Take what they say with a grain of salt and adjust the parts that you agree with.

Day 20

Have children read your story, or read it to them.

Do they stay interested? Are they silent or are they hounding you with questions?

Ask them how they would improve it.

Hone your story even more.

Day 21

Take a break from writing and look in your local yellow pages for editors and proof-readers.

Pick one that has specific experience with this type of editing, and have him or her professionally edit your work. Ask them for a critique as well.

Day 22

Make your final corrections.

Pull out the list of editors and publishers from your first few days of research.

Write a cover letter (query letter) that will go to each editor/proofreader, or hire a professional copywriter to do so for you.

Keep it professional. No cutesy remarks. No flowery paper. No talking about how this has been your lifelong dream. Stick to what your book is about and how it fills a need for them.

Day 23

Go online and print out form TX from the Copyright Office.

Send in the completed form and a copy of your book with the required $30 fee.

Relax for the rest of the day with your family and friends.

Day 24

Print out 10 copies of your manuscript on quality white computer paper.

Do not staple your pages together! Keep them bound with a paper clip in the corner.

Keep them ready to send out once an editor requests your manuscript.

Make sure to write an editor's name on each cover letter and envelope.

Include Self Addressed Stamped Envelopes (SASEs) for return!

Days 25-30

Send query letters out to editors until you receive a positive response, or review my section on SELF-PUBLISHING.

Remember: persistence counts.

If you do decide to self-publish, remember to send out your press releases, as explained in CREATING A MAR-KETING PLAN.

ABOUT THE AUTHOR

Caterina Christakos is a successful actress and model. In addition to starring in the feature film "Alone and Restless" and modeling for companies like Physique and Sephora, Caterina is also a published author and a radio announcer.

Caterina's books include:

And Dreams Lost Along the Way
- a children's book about rediscovering dreams

If I Could Remember All the Things She Forgot
- a tribute to grandmothers everywhere

How to Completely Blow Your Competition Away at Any Audition
- the complete guide to auditioning for acting and modeling
  jobs

She has also had articles published in <u>Accent on Living Magazine</u> and <u>Active Living Magazine</u>.

0-595-26260-0

Printed in the United States
46451LVS00006B/418-426